inspired?
get writing!

More new poems and short stories
inspired by the collection of the
National Galleries of Scotland

National Galleries of Scotland

*in association with the Scottish Poetry Library
and the English-Speaking Union Scotland*

A NOTE ON THE CATEGORIES

The entries are accompanied by a note indicating into which category they were entered:

CATEGORY A   under 12 years
CATEGORY B   12 – 15 years
CATEGORY C   16 – 18 years
CATEGORY D   unpublished adults
CATEGORY E   published adults

Published by the Trustees of the
National Galleries of Scotland 2009

ISBN 978 1 906270 24 7

Designed by Dalrymple
Typeset in Verdigris and Modern no.20
Printed on Chromomatt 150gsm by Nicholson & Bass

National Galleries of Scotland is a charity registered
in Scotland no.SC003728

www.nationalgalleries.org

Foreword

The *inspired? get writing!* creative writing competition is a major event in the calendars of its participating organisations: the National Galleries of Scotland, the English-Speaking Union Scotland and the Scottish Poetry Library. The competition which was launched in 2005 is now in its fourth successful year, and this is the second anthology of winning entries. Originally devised to raise awareness of the National Galleries of Scotland's collection, the competition aims to encourage writers to find imaginative links, from the personal to the universal, between art and the written word.

In 2006 and 2007 there was generous sponsorship and support from the Scottish Qualifications Authority, and in 2008, from the Gordon Fraser Charitable Trust and the Scottish Arts Council. Due to funding from the Educational Institute for Scotland and valuable publicity provided by *The Scotsman*, which published the winning entries, we have been able to hold creative writing tours and workshops for our young winners, led by professional artists and writers.

Cross-fertilisation has long existed in the arts; great art has been inspired by literature, and great literature has reflected on and interpreted visual art. In education today, the Curriculum for Excellence endorses the arts as a powerful medium for cross-curricular learning. This anthology celebrates these connections and the links between people and art: the act of seeing, feeling, finding – and sharing – words.

It showcases the winning works from 2008 and 2009 and, we hope, will engage, surprise and delight a wide readership, and show them something of the diversity of the national collection. Each year the winners, their families, friends, and the wider public, can share in the celebration by attending the annual awards ceremony and readings events at the National Galleries of Scotland in Edinburgh.

We wish to thank wholeheartedly the judges, sponsors and supporters who have helped to make the competition and this anthology possible. We extend this gratitude to the organisers who endeavour to build the competition and ensure its future: Linda McClelland (National Galleries of Scotland), John Duncan and Suzanne Ensom (English-Speaking Union Scotland), and Lorna Irvine (Scottish Poetry Library). Above all, we applaud all the entrants, for their involvement, enthusiasm and words, and we invite each of you to lift your pens to enter the next *inspired? get writing!* competition.

JOHN LEIGHTON
Director-General, National Galleries of Scotland

JON DYE
Chairman, English-Speaking Union Scotland

ROBYN MARSACK
Director, Scottish Poetry Library

Janice Galloway

A Way of Seeing

There's a story about L.S. Lowry, the famous renderer of so-called 'industrial scenes'. Lowry, a man 'enraptured' by what he found before him in everyday Manchester and its environs – 'the huge black framework of rows of yellow-lit windows standing up against the sad, damp charged afternoon sky, the mill turning out' – was not far-travelled. He never saw the need. Late in life, however, he was befriended by a couple who wished to expose the elderly painter to the riotously floral landscapes of southern France. For whatever reason, Lowry agreed. Day after day, the benefactors watched the old man wander to the bottom of a sunflower field, paints in hand, and tried to restrain their excitement. After a lifetime of monochrome, surely the great man's ideas would be stirred? Revolutionised? Eventually, unable to restrain their curiosity any longer, they approached the artist as he worked, hatless, under a tree and peeked over his shoulder. Lowry was painting – an industrial landscape.

What the benefactors had forgotten, perhaps never knew, is that an artist is not a camera. What the artist does, even in the most lifelike of work, is *more than* a literal tableau. The artist invites us into not *what is seen*, but a *way of seeing*. Lowry was a man so practised in his vision that it remained his key to meaning, his message, even when shown something ostensibly and overtly very different. Children, those lucky/young enough to remain uncluttered by common expectation, do exactly the same. The puzzled adult's 'what is it?' when confronted by a two-year-old's abstract is beside the point. It's *the moment*, not the detail of what is present, that matters. Van Gogh, an artist who painted those very sunflower fields Lowry saw years later, did not render their conventional beauty either, but the sea-waves and bonfires of near-uncontrollable inner life. Would Van Gogh's work have been revolutionised by a trip to Lowry's home town? I doubt it. His way of seeing, like Lowry's, like that of all great artists in whatever field, is directed from inner, not outward, vision.

What you will find between the pages of this beautifully illustrated book are similar encounters: writers asked to engage with the National Galleries' wide-ranging collection, and gift us that encounter through the medium not of paint, but words.

How the subject matter spoke to them as individuals is strikingly varied, even when they reflect the same source of inspiration. Some of the authors chose to see from inside, effectively *becoming* the subjects represented in the artwork. The abstract confection of *Mr Peanut* or the short and witty *Composition 14*, the daintily observed *The Lady in the Picture* and gentle *Niel Gow* certainly fall into this category. Others, like the author of *Life Class*, or the startlingly confrontational *Highland Coo*, become poet-as-onlooker, seeing the subject caught in the moment, a fellow-creature that might answer back, turn, notice them in return at any moment. Others again are moved to extend their empathy to the painter himself, as in the rich, multi-layered world of *The Buried Sun*, or the tender voyeurism of *A Woman in Bed*, where Rembrandt's personal compassion and insight inspires wonderful glimpses of strong, inner lives.

Portraits provided rich pickings – the passionate portrait of Jennie Lee, or the openness of Bellany's *My Father* spring to mind; while for other writers, the picture acts as a springboard for imagination, speculation and fabulous fantasy – read the heavily sensual *Adam*, the weirdly compelling *The Green Cactus* or *Ship of Women*'s bravura surreality married to startling powers of down-to-earth description, and you'll see what I mean. Throughout, the approaches and tacks are subtle, various, and wide-ranging enough to evidence that art inspires art and always will.

From the sound-inflected empathy of *The Wave* – a perfect showcase of sustenance from sculpture – to *Forgetting*, which spins a scrawny sketch into textured personal reflection; from *125th and Lenox*, extemporising freely on its jazzy inspiration, to the startling off-kilter steadfastness of *How Jane Wilson Steadied the World on her Long Walk Home from School*; from *La Femme au Parapluie*'s astonishing expansion from source into the inner life of a sexual obsessive to – well, I could go on but you doubtless have the gist. Read them *all* for yourselves, bracketing the words with the original vision, enriching your own insights into the bargain. Art is a collaborative process or it is mere howling at the moon. Here are clear, direct voices, offering visions, ways of seeing, in pairs. All you have to do is look.

Niel Gow (1727–1807)
by Sir Henry Raeburn

by JESSAMY COWIE

A wise, travelled face. Frozen in time. I stare from my frame, at all the busy people, passing me with hardly a backwards glance. Their eyes pass over me, looking at me but seeing only a common painting despite the master who portrayed me. Perhaps if they took some time to look at me properly, they would see my life story etched on my ruddy face and hear the music in my heart. I hold my fiddle in my hand, the bow paused mid note. It is my most treasured possession. Its jaunty reels and sad laments are but a memory now. The Strathspeys I wrote have seen 200 years. The last ghostly tendrils of fiddle music weave through my head as I watch you admire me fleetingly before moving on to my neighbour.
Please stay a while.

[CATEGORY A]

SIR HENRY RAEBURN
Niel Gow (1727–1807), 1787
PG 160 · purchased 1886

Sun Worship

by CALUM GARDNER

The brave youth flirts outrageously with Dawn
She squeals and flees into the falling east.
Past Morning, tempering her frosty fervour
He makes his way to Noon. On, noble steed!
He strains to climb the great dome's peak, and we,
We feel it too. We sweat and swoon for Him,
And with our help, He tricks us, ties us up,
Our shadows lashed onto His chariot
We watch, helpless, as they are dragged into
The underworld, and measured for our chains.
We restless citizens, we look above
And therefore think we know all our solutions;
But He is doing what we should have done
He's setting our metropolis on fire.

[CATEGORY C]

DAVID ROBERTS

Rome: Sunset from the Convent of Sant' Onofrio on the Janiculum, 1856

NG 304 · presented by the artist to the Royal Scottish Academy 1857;
transferred to the National Gallery of Scotland 1910

The Buried Sun

by IAN McDONOUGH

Aged two, they said, I drew the outline of a sparrow in the dirt.
Soon my eye consumed the whole of Leyden,
fingers etched with light, ears burning
with a score of crafty secrets from old Swanenburch,
Pieter Lastmann's recipe for clouds.

Fast enough I left them, the old devils, to their tricks,
set off to snare the glory of our world. Year on year,
rejoicing, aching, among gesso chalk and glue,
layering imprimatura till my boards yielded such glow
you'd swear the sun lay buried just beneath the floor.

Older, I turned rougher with the brush, capturing
nothing more or less than I bore witness to.
This blanket of years, sewing such a bleak embroidery,
presses heavy as time rolls, stifling the blaze to smoulders,
Ochre to Raw Umber, then the frightful edges of Bone Black.

[CATEGORY E]

REMBRANDT VAN RIJN
Self-portrait, aged 51, c.1657
NGL 072.46 · Edinburgh, National Gallery of
Scotland (Bridgewater Loan, 1945)

Mr Peanut

by GEORGIA GAGE

Floating around, who knows what odd
and unnatural images will stir a long forgotten
memory. For each story a little trinket lies
behind it. For each little trinket, a story lies before it.

That time when the brother was accused for the missing
chocolate bar. As a semi-eaten 'crunchy' sails by.
You remember.

Or the missing prize pineapple from the Modbury
fruit and produce show on the 2nd of July, Devon.
You remember.

That fatal time when the heart of a frail patient vanished
from the operating theatre. A life gone, lost, forgotten.
Given to the world of the forgotten, lost and gone.
Suspended in limbo.
You remember.

'Mr Peanut' still dances on the piece of paper cut
from the packet. Gone, lost, forgotten.
You forget.

[CATEGORY B]

EDUARDO PAOLOZZI
Mr Peanut, 1970
GMA 4051 · bequest of Gabrielle Keiller 1995

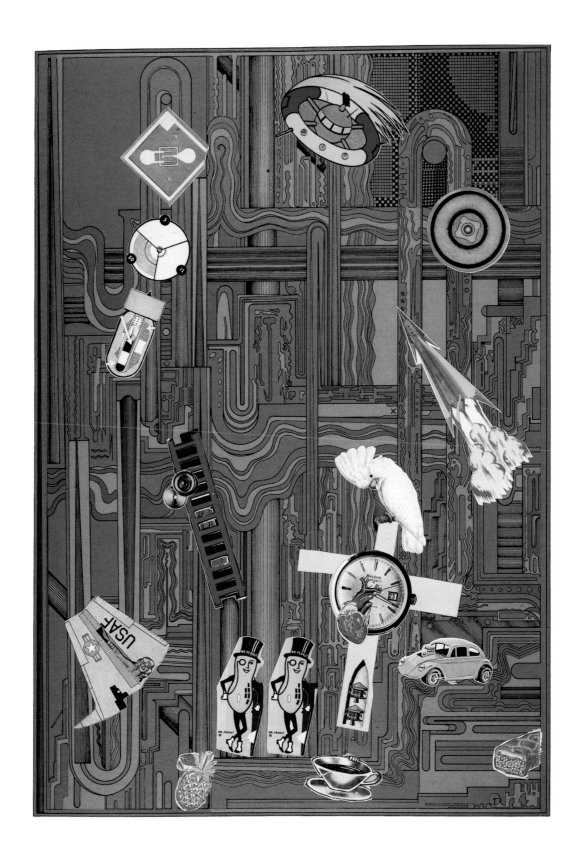

Ship of Women

by JOHN JENNETT

My mother was a great spoon of a woman who had a terrible fear of fish. This had come about because she had once been travelling with her father and they had been late for the tide. The driver said he would get them over but as soon as the wheels of the cart sliced the muddy sand and the horses started to splash in the shallows, a wind came up from the West and piled the sea quickly up on top of the tide.

Of the two horses one was an old hand but the young mare, who was milked every day to feed the coachman's motherless son, took fright. The cart was twisting off the ground as the horse reared and the mare's eyes were as white as the waves that were starting to hiss around the cart. The driver was a quick-thinking man and he cut the young horse free right in the middle of the channel and without a backwards look to see where it had gone, shouted the old horse to pull them on.

The coast was patrolled by a thousand salmon that day, all heavy with spawn. They were eager for the end of the ebb and as they sensed the turn of the tide the shoal had plunged towards the land. When the king of fish found their way blocked by the cart and the wild horse they all tried to leap clear of the obstruction, pressing on for the place where they would abandon their eggs and die.

The air filled with my mother's screams, as the cart emerged safely on the other side of the sound with the water pouring off it. According to the coachman she had a dozen muscular salmon writhing around in her skirts. My mother did not talk for a month and never again ate a fish or would allow one in the house. She made a noise like a horse if she got so much as a splash of water on her head. My sister would never say what happened when she remained alone with her, on the last Sunday of every month, to help wash her hair.

Our township had three houses and two women apart from my mother. Joy always seemed to be pregnant but I never saw her with a baby. Over the years she took on the appearance of an infant herself, losing her hair and developing thick cheeks

WILL MACLEAN
Bard McIntyre's Box, 1984
GMA 2973 · purchased 1986

In addition to *Bard McIntyre's Box*, this piece is partly inspired by an autobiographical fragment in C. Hall, *To the Edge of the Sea*, Edinburgh, 1999, p.5, which describes a lifelong fear of water by an island woman following a dangerous tidal crossing. This is otherwise a work of fiction. All characters and events are the production of the author's imagination.

and a round face that was as blue as robin's egg. I've always thought that Ada, the other woman, resembles a frog and she smells tarry as if she's been left too long in the oven. Ada didn't like talking to Mum when I was in the room.

'A word in your shell-like, Fay?' is what she would say to her, raising her eyebrows and twitching her froggy head in the direction of the next room.

When war was declared all the men went away and the women were left in charge of the island. May came around, the wind set in the East and it was time to cut peats for the next winter. After wrestling the sheep in August to strip them of their fleeces, the three women were hardy enough for the job and it was months since my mother had stopped gouging the earth out from under her nails.

What made her pale and grumpy was the place where the peats were, on the other side of the water. You couldn't go round the top of the loch because that was bad luck going away from the sun and you couldn't go round the bottom because the sea was there.

The three women contemplated the upturned clinker boat, hauled up after last year's peats had come home. My mother prowled around the old skiff. She was the leader, of course, but was quite beside herself with fear. Even Ada was worried about water-horses. They decided to heave the boat right way up on dry land and have a go at rowing it there. When they turned it up they found two fat shelduck sleeping underneath it. Joy wrang their necks; Ada said it was bad luck and my mother shivered.

For a week my mother directed the other women to sit in the boat twenty yards from the water and thread the long painted oars through the holes. When they tired of falling backwards with no water to push against, their thoughts turned to weapons to deal with whatever they encountered. My mother's main concern was the fish and she asked the other women what they might bring.

Joy's husband was a forester and she brought along a big beater that he used for slapping out fires. Ada took the crook that she had been given with instructions to control Angus, the bull, during the war. Reluctantly my mother said fine they must go if they were not all to freeze to death in the winter.

The day they pushed off out the shallows, the water lilies were starting to show and Joy said the loch was so calm that a midge could take a drink from it. My mother stood in the middle of the boat whilst the other women puffed away at the rowing but when she saw the surface of the loch pucker she was so terrified that she asked the women to ship their oars and hand their weapons.

The enemy in the war was fond of submarines and it was many years before we found out what really happened that day. They say that when the captain looked through his periscope as the submarine rose up he felt his neck turn cold. He had just been marvelling at how rich this water was with fish but he caught a glimpse of a boat carrying three witches. Three women was bad luck in his country too.

'Ship of Women, Ship of women!' he cried and without an order the helm made the submarine glide back underneath so that the periscope had barely broken through. The women's boat had rocked gently from the little ripple that seemed to have come from nowhere.

'Shouldn't have killed the ducks,' muttered Ada.

Even though the wave was tiny the story goes that my mother toppled right out of the boat. Her friends, strong from the sheep, were able to fish her quickly from the sea but they had heard her hit her head on something so hard it sounded like metal.

My mother was dead and the sea-pinks were still fresh on her grave when the war was over.

[CATEGORY D]

WILL MACLEAN
Detail from *Bard McIntyre's Box*, 1984
GMA 2973 · purchased 1986

21

My Biological Dwelling

by TAYLOR WATSON-FARGIE

Am I being preserved in this womb of dull green cells?
Do these cells contain golden necessities or fetid fiends?
What am I? – A pilgrim, a saviour, a foetus?
A tunnel to rest in?
This is Shangri-La, an antediluvian innovation…
It is a chamber as old as history.

All around me, fibres like hair, soft and luscious –
Flow and meander along this outer cell of my domain.
They originate and form a mass of grotesquely MiShApEn entities like globe-stones
eroded by ferocious seas.

All-around my halo, echo serrated-supernovas,
They twang with mechanical uncertainty
Like daggers thrust into a metallic green cosmos,
Like orphans wondering who they belong to.
These celestial demons emit life into the skies.

I am lost forever in this biological cave –
what life?

Why am I here?

[CATEGORY B]

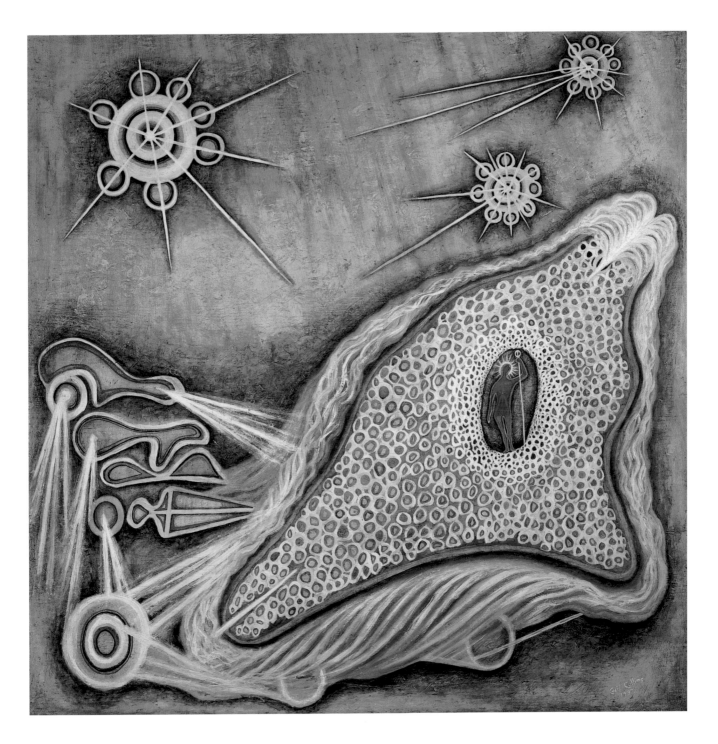

CECIL COLLINS

The Joy of the Worlds, 1937

GMA 4372 · bequest of Mrs Elisabeth Collins
through The Art Fund 2001

The Wave

by MORGAN DOWNIE

when the wave came
white eyed,
it left behind its heart
discarded, broken
an object for which
it had no more use
strange wood
to be found
by the beach walker
who had never
seen its like before

he sharpened
his carving tools
closed his eyes
and let the
wounded grain
find shape
under his hands
he polished it
with the fat
of gannets,
half blind
with the stink,
rubbed it smooth
with the vanes
of flight feathers
he strung the wood
with fibres of drift nets,
tuned to kelp harmonics
tidal scordatura
intricate as coral
until in the strings
he heard the sea

he went to the headland
out over the grieving waters
he played the voice
of wingborne gulls
the restless sigh
of dune grass
sand hissing
in autumnal gales
he played until
the sea was quiet
he played until
he was stone
he played until
the wave came
and gentle
washed around him

[CATEGORY E]

GEORGE WILSON

A Fallen Beech Tree, 1880

D 5023.48 · bequest of Miss Helen Barlow 1976

La Femme au Parapluie

by LUCY HALL

She was the only dash of colour in her monochromatic world. She was like a lick of red paint that marked a pathway through the crowding umbrellas. They hovered over her, the reflective sheen of wet material bobbing and ducking like waves. Her red dress was drowning, oppressed beneath the ocean of black.

Rain shimmered, a misty veil over the city making the grey stone buildings almost glisten in the dull twilight. Blurs of orange and yellow floated in hazy orbs over the hustle and bustle of the street. Each was like its own sunset, burning through the rain and smog. The red dress darted onwards, battling against the current of murky umbrellas and oblivious to the poetry she created. Oblivious…

She stopped, a space forming around her. The crowd parted. The rain seemed to slow where she stood. While the torrent of icy droplets pierced the skin of those around – calm surrounded her. She was the eye of the storm. Anything that existed beyond her was chaos. A disorganised clamour for attention. White noise.

Like a weapon she brandished a red umbrella against the storm. Time slowed as she extended her yellow leather glove from the confines of her sleeve. Delicate fingers grasped the hooked handle while her other hand caressed the length of the wood. A plumage of red burst open, exploding and scattering the dreary black that surrounded her. A firework against the autumn sky. And now her splash of red joined the sea as she raised it overhead.

A businesslike flick of her black curls, miraculously dry.

She stood elegantly on the kerbside waiting for a gap in the cars, the toes of her yellow button-up boots overhanging, creasing as she swayed and swung to and fro carried by the wind. She searched for a crossing. The fluid black taxi cabs wailed, competing with the roar of the rain. They brashly thundered by her, kicking up spray from the roadside that scattered and settled on her red dress like fragments of dust. Foul, brazen beasts – they clattered by, bumpers almost touching, hassled in the heavy traffic – and would not let her pass. They formed a wall between the parallel pavements.

A sprightly skip and a graceful leap, the red dress bounced neatly over the tarmac avoiding puddles and raindrops. She floated, the hem of her red dress fluttering behind her. Soles of her yellow boots seemed not to be tarnished by touching the ground, she walked on water.

He battled against the harsh wind that corroded his cheeks and swept the breath from his lungs. Rain blinded him, his spectacles clouding and crystal droplets weighing down his exposed hair. He darted amidst the forest of umbrellas that moaned and shook unsteadily. Now that she was gone the storm had worsened, punishing the world for being incomparable to the splendour of the woman in the red dress. *His* woman in the red dress…

Lurching, stumbling through the crowds he fought onwards, his trail mapped out clearly by red among the black and imprinted on his inner-eye. The rain surged and the desert that was his heavy tweed coat drank it up eagerly. And still he continued. Tripping over his own large feet, wading through puddles – he would never be as graceful as she. The black curtain of night was falling keenly, shrouding the city in a twilight that buzzed with endless fluorescent lights. It was trivial. Jostled by the masses, he was carried forward by the course of the crowd and the wind. A short pause to slide the round spectacles up the bridge of his nose before they could plummet towards the slick pavement beneath his clumsy footing.

He stopped at the doorway and removed the glasses that encircled his weary green eyes. The cuff of his coat swept rashly over the lenses, moving smears of rain to new areas and he carefully aligned them once more on his thin nose. There was no other occasion that caused such a desire within him to appear presentable. But this was his ritual. With pleasure he completed it by combing his fingers hastily through his

MAX ERNST
La Femme au parapluie
(Woman with Umbrella),
*c.*1921
GMA 3970 · bequest of
Gabrielle Keiller 1995

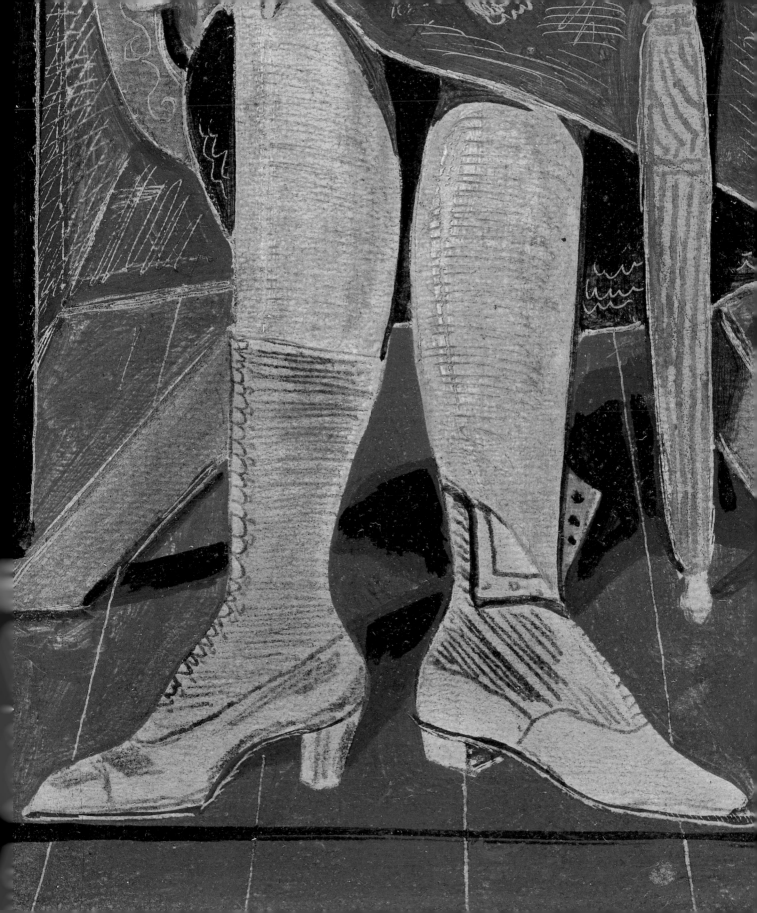

hair, soaked black by the rain, and checking his appearance in the window. Nervous fingers fumbled, jamming a graceful cigarette between his thin lips, pursed with concentration. A click and a flicker of the flame. Grey smoke rose in the damp air, the steady glow from the end of his cigarette pulsating in the dark as he waited. Listening to the gradual taming of the rain and the drip of broken guttering.

And she emerged. Her red dress dancing about her knees like fire. With her damp black curls licking her cheekbones and her heeled boots tapping the kitchen tiles. He could not hear the rhythmic beat of her steps, but he could imagine it. Just as he could imagine the soft scraping of the wooden stool legs being dragged from beneath the table. Just as he could imagine the sigh of exhausted relief that floated from her lips as she sat, removing the weight from her feet.

His breath puffed hot clouds into the air, mingled with the thick fog of cigarette smoke, misting the glass of the window dreamily.

There was no movement from within, as there was no movement where he stood. But he was enthralled.

Finally she stirred from her leisurely sprawl and began peeling the yellow leather gloves from her hands; slowly working the fabric from each delicate fingertip, taking great care not to stretch the soft material.

The musty smell of new leather lingered in his nostrils as he drew in deeper breaths of tobacco.

She discarded them limply on the kitchen table as though they meant nothing to her; as though they were so easily replaced.

He could hear the oh-so quiet creak of her boots echoing, silently, in his ear as she ruthlessly pulled the material over each of the buttons that bound the shoe around her beautifully crafted ankle.

It was only he who noticed the smallest actions which made her so wonderful. She appeared as a dream, moving with elegance on the other side of the hazy glass. To think, the only barrier that kept them apart was that thin, transparent window pane – it thrilled him. There was always that prowling danger that caused his heart to thunder in his chest and the terror that lurked at the back of his mind to flutter frantically with almost unbearable excitement. Part of him desired, so deeply, for her to notice. To catch a fleeting glimpse of his bedraggled figure, hovering in the corner of her eye.

But that would shatter the illusion, the fantasy, he had of her.

And that would ruin everything.

[CATEGORY C]

MAX ERNST
Detail from *La Femme au parapluie (Woman with Umbrella)*, *c.1921*
GMA 3970 · bequest of Gabrielle Keiller 1995

41

Le Drapeau Noir

by PHOEBE FISHER

They come at night, soaring,
Swooping, sneaking
Over towns and cities.
They shelter in shadows, hiding,
Birds of the night.
Their dark painted sides glint
Dully, as they creep closer,
An invading army of vultures, waiting
For a kill.

They come and leave in silence,
Gliding away as the dawn approaches,
Following pathways and shining white roads,
Reflected in the moonlight, always flying
In purposeful circles, never lost.

They leave nothing but a memory
For the ripples of the imagination
That grow to a peak in the darkness.
But listen and be warned,
They will come at night, soaring.
Beware.

[CATEGORY B]

RENE MAGRITTE
Le Drapeau noir (The Black Flag), 1937
GMA 1261 · purchased 1972

Midnight Spin

by ROXANNE PARIS

Come by. Take me out tonight.
Pick me up in the one I like.
I will wait for you on the rooftop
playing connect the dots
with Sirius and Dione.
We can circle the city,
lights below our toes
like incandescent ants.
I will hang my head
out the window
inhaling dusk
exhaling gravity.

[CATEGORY D]

RENE MAGRITTE
Detail from *Le Drapeau noir (The Black Flag)*, 1937
GMA 1261 · purchased 1972

Jennie Lee by Robert Capa

by ANDY JACKSON

Daughters, hear the truth. Back then,
no pit was deep enough for diamonds,
none would strike a match
for fear of fire-damp.
The roar of the conveyor belt
drove girls from blackened homes
in Fife, their coughing fathers
burning out like cinders.

She was caught by gales that swept
across the steppes, to rattle windows
on collective farms, yearning for
the gusts of revolution.
She broke the ceilings in a ruin,
breathed on plaster till it cracked,
then helped to mix the sand
with the cement to build us up again.

The artist, bleak in his fatigues
and listening out for shells,
is sizing up the shot. His art
is in the truth, his propaganda
is the likeness of a better world
already here, if we could only see
its levelling of light and dark,
its socialism of the eye.

[CATEGORY D]

ROBERT CAPA

Jennie Lee, Independent Socialist Candidate,
Bristol Central By-election, 1943

PGP 253.1 · purchased 1999

The Bogeyman

by SANDI AITCHISON

He crouches outside your window,
Watching, waiting for the sound of
Footsteps, for the light to click
Off.
Then he rises like smoke,
To pour through the glass.

When he stands at the end
Of your bed,
You twitch in your sleep,
For you know, inside, he is there.
He laughs as he watches your
Dreams turn to ashes and the
Darkness touches your mind.

As you wake, at the end
Of your bed, you might see,
A gentleman. Who smiles at you,
A flash of blades beneath
His lips and when he tips his
Hat, *Good evening*, you glimpse
The daggers at the end of his hand.

As he lets himself into the
Closet, he looks back at you
And chuckles, when you ask for his name,
He winks, calls you darling and says,
I'll be back tomorrow, young miss.

[CATEGORY C]

Highland Coo

by NILES GOURLAY

In the bonny
Highlands
a coo
stands in the mud
wet as seaweed.
Ets horns ur
as smooth as
silk
and it stares
at me.

Its hair is as
lang as Liam's
he's all alane here
and naeone ta
keep im company

He looks like he's
came oot of the
mud
and disnay look
angry.
I look at him
He disny ken.

[CATEGORY A]

BILL BRANDT
Loch Slapin, Isle of Skye, 1947
PGP 254.2 · purchased 2000

How Jane Wilson Steadied the World on her Long Walk Home from School

by ALAN GAY

Still dizzy from flu, longing
for her mother's hot kitchen,
seven year old Jane Wilson's legs ache
from pushing through deep snow.

A low moon flicks on and off
through pastel painted clouds
making trees leap, the barn stagger –
throw shadows at her.

The brae ahead leans to the right
sending the village down the slope
to pile into a writhing sea beyond.
Telegraph poles totter.
Bonfires in the trees spin.

She finds that by tilting her head
well to the left and concentrating hard
she can halt the slide, hold the village level.
Cottages now stand upright.
Hot scones shuffle back on to stoves.

A pointed finger commands
telegraph poles back in line.
Waving her handkerchief thus,
drives aside the barn's menace.

A loud sneeze followed by Jane's hard stare
so shocks the moon, it stops its tricks
to beam constant on the last mile home.

[CATEGORY E]

52

JOAN EARDLEY
Catterline in Winter, 1963
GMA 888 · purchased 1964

The Green Cactus

by DENIS McCANCE

The green cactus is bright as water
It hangs like a swing
And eleven men, dirty as pigs,
passing iron like pass-the-parcel.

Wiggly clouds like fish in the sea

The pirate crew with jobs to do
Climbing up the crow's nest
Like dogs trying to get up the tree

We fight all night to get back on the sea
but we need a drink
We work very hard
but we need to get on the sea
We need to get off this hairy, scary island.
The green cactus will save us all
With fresh water inside.

[CATEGORY A]

FERNAND LÉGER
Etude pour 'Les Constructeurs': l'équipe au repos
(Study for 'The Constructors': The Team at Rest), 1950
GMA 2845 · purchased 1984

A Woman in Bed

by PHILIPPA CARTER

Some days he thought he couldn't bear it. He would remember it all, he would remember again the starched bed linen blossoming scarlet beneath him, the endless weeping, the impossible waxing and waning of belly and breast. It was senseless to him, beyond comprehension. And then back, back painfully further still, to the day of his wedding, staring at that young girl with petals caught in the pale flax of her hair.

The mystery of it had been of such rapture to him, then, such an imminent promise of perfection. He would imagine entering his wife, no, being her, feeling the words vibrate soft between teeth and tongue, seeing those small feet while washing, knowing the foreign warmth of her body in place of his own. Even the paintings haunted him now. Saskia as Flora, Saskia with that flushed, half self-conscious smile. He couldn't bear to have the damned things in the studio and screamed curses at anyone who mentioned removing them.

How could it be that the events of so many years ago could still be like this in his mind, like a new wound, like fresh paint? This world that he loved so dearly, this nature, his mistress, his best and oldest lover, had played a trick on him so cruel that even now he could find no reconciliation for it. He had watched that pink young woman grow aged and weathered next to him, slowly, gently, in his mind's eye. But there was no way of making sense of the things that never were, of the days that never happened. There had been no explanation, not a thing left as evidence but a side of the bed left always clean and unslept in.

It was still that same bed, in the house on the Jodenbreestrat. The place itself, the room, the worn finery, was so familiar to him it had ceased to be painful, like a pair of costly shoes that had never quite fitted. But this creature lying inside was the anomaly. He had walked in on her while bathing at first, accidentally. He'd only caught a sudden glimpse, of white thighs tapering out of the water like candle wax, of hair curling

64

REMBRANDT VAN RIJN
A Woman in Bed, *c.*1645–6
NG 827 · presented by William McEwan 1892

Index